# How to make little kids listen:

## A Guide for good parenting

Victoria McLean

# Table of contents

# Chapter 1

How to help your children manage their emotions?

Children are more in need than ever of attention to their mental well-being during challenging times. You may have observed certain classes this year at your children's school that are centered on emotions as a result. Social-emotional learning, or SEL, is what many instructors used to assist pupils in adjusting to the significant changes that the year 2020 brought.

Learning how to handle stress may assist, additionally, pupils feel a stronger connection to their instructors when SEL skills are taught in the classroom. You shouldn't be concerned even if your child's school doesn't teach SEL skills. The good news is that kids can learn SEL at home with your assistance.

What is **SEL**?

At its most basic level, SEL is a series of techniques for teaching kids or adults how to control their emotions and form good relationships with others. James Comer, a child psychiatrist, first proposed the concept in the 1960s, arguing that underprivileged pupils would do better academically if they felt more appreciated and safe at school.

He created a prototype program at the Yale School of Medicine's Child Study Center, launched it at two New Haven schools with poor academic achievement, and observed as behavioral concerns decreased and academic performance improved.

By the 1990s, hundreds of schools were offering SEL courses, and in 1995, Daniel Goleman's best-seller Emotional Intelligence helped popularize the term.

Standards for social and emotional learning are now accepted in educational institutions all across the globe. Sarna teaches SEL courses as separate units, but instructors may also incorporate them into academic classes by asking and responding to insightful questions and comments. Lessons like recognizing and labeling emotions, having empathy for others, and learning how to form positive connections are all meant to help students develop life skills.

How does **SEL** aid?

While taking a break from academics to discuss emotions may seem counterproductive for learning, more than 20 years of study have shown that doing so can improve academic achievement, improve mental health, lower dropout rates, and more. Kids do better when they feel better, after all.

According to a Pennsylvania State University study that followed kindergarteners until they were 25 years old, those who displayed "prosocial behavior" early on had a higher likelihood of not getting into trouble with the law, abstaining from drugs and alcohol, and maintaining good mental health as adults. These abilities may also be taught.

Children who engaged in SEL programs had better classroom behavior, were better at managing their stress, and scored 11 percentile points higher in academics than children who did not participate in SEL programs, according to a study of research involving more than 270,000 pupils.

How can **SEL** be done at home?

Whether or not your children are learning about SEL at school, they might need a little additional help during these trying times. Here are some quick and easy SEL activities you can do at home with your children to reap some of the same advantages.

- **Draw air from your belly**: We utilize this skill, according to Sarna, "to quiet down powerful emotions, or when youngsters feel they can't concentrate, or when they need to calm distractions." Children breathe in through their nostrils while placing their hands on their stomachs. They should breathe "like they're tasting excellent soup," you may tell them. Encourage them to feel the air entering their lungs. Then tell them to exhale as if they are cooling the soup. Before responding to a situation or sitting down to finish their schoolwork, children might "take a belly breath."

- **Create a family compass**: According to Cipriano, "This is a paper you associate with your family or with your classroom unit." Cipriano and her family came up with their charter at the start of the pandemic: "We asked, 'How do we want to feel in this home, and what will we do to feel this way?'" The family of Cipriano has determined that they all want to be treated with respect and heard. They later came up with ideas on how to get there and wrote, "We'll pay attention to what others say and don't say. She advises sitting down with your children and asking them to brainstorm four or five adjectives that best describe the feelings they want to experience, followed by four or five actions that they can all agree to undertake to get there.

- **Exchange thorns and flowers**: Ask the family, "What was anything wonderful that occurred today?" before you sat down to dinner. "Let's discuss a challenge from our day," was the next command. The difficulties are the thorns, while the advantages are the flowers. Keep your impulse to provide a solution at bay when someone shares a thorn. How did you manage it is a question you may ask. says VanAusdal. "Or, if the conflict persists, ask yourself, "What can we do collectively to assist us to move through that difficulty? Give children the opportunity to think critically and use their problem-solving skills."

- **Count to three**: Sarna believes that it is effective to allow children three minutes to think and do nothing. Instead of bombarding youngsters with information we already know, "just giving them the freedom to ponder, letting their minds go wild, helps them to tap into their intuition."

- **Examine a mood meter**: This is a list of emotions that children may use to describe their feelings at any time, such as before an exam, after a challenging day, or even during a tantrum. Cipriano claims that it aids in more accurate emotion identification "and it increases self-awareness so that we may learn to control by acknowledging and expressing our feelings. She claims that if children can identify their emotions, they may utilize that knowledge to make better judgments that aren't entirely influenced by feelings. Both a mood meter app and a free printed version are available here.

- **Reading aloud to younger children**: When telling a narrative, you could pause to consider: 'How did that character manage this conflict? What gives this character such powerful qualities? Why did this obstacle arise? vanAusdal recommends. It helps young children develop a vocabulary for their emotions.

- **Express your emotions**: When Sarna asks a class, "Who has ever felt scared?" sometimes no one responds, she explains. I follow up by saying, "Well, I've been afraid. Then, everyone tries to claim that they were alarmed. Everyone feels a bit cozier now. He claims that through expressing emotion, they might learn that their sentiments are normal.


- **Beat a drum**: Cipriano explains, "We call this taking a meta-moment." When something occurs or you feel something, you pause and ask yourself, "What would my best self do in this situation?" before acting. Whatever your best self would do before jumping to a decision, you carry out. So a youngster may declare, "I'm feeling irritated right now," in the heat of the moment. I'm now experiencing fury. What would I do if I were myself in this circumstance? Cipriano argues that both adults and children may benefit from this in understanding the connection between our emotions and actions.

# Chapter 2

How to resolve conflict with your  children

Because conflict will always arise in life, we must teach our children coping mechanisms for handling divergent viewpoints. As they become older, our kids can negotiate the playground and later the job with the aid of conflict resolution skills.

The teaching of constructive means of resolving disputes to kids is a natural component of primary education. As any parent of several children can attest, children do not automatically know how to interact with people when they are born. Ensuring that instructors provide their pupils with the knowledge and skills necessary to make wise choices and resolve interpersonal problems is a key component of basic education.

This often entails some kind of appeal to the teacher's authority in the traditional classroom. When a student has a problem, the instructor steps in like a judge to administer justice from above.

**Stop, Talk With Others, and Listen**

Teaching children to take a moment to calm down after being upset is one of the most basic strategies employed, and it is something that can be done at home with ease. Although anger is a normal reaction to disagreement, it makes it challenging to process feelings and develop a constructive strategy for settlement.

Adults may comprehend it with ease, but kids may not see it as clearly. Before being instructed to consider what the disagreement was that they were engaged in, students are advised to detach and clear their minds. Instead of merely focusing on the fact that they are furious, they should consider why.

**The Resolution Table for Conflict**

Children are encouraged to express the emotional component of their argument in very specific language once they have calmed down rather than waiting for the instructor to pass judgment. Encourage them to express their dilemma using the pronouns "I think that," "I feel," or "I wish" and to focus only on how the dispute made them feel. Just their interpretation of the conflict's character, without any judgment. Students can distinguish between the conflict's emotional component and their comprehension of it by considering their point of view.

Both parties may sit down at the conflict resolution table after they have both had a chance to collect themselves and identify their problems. Students express their issues succinctly and in language that relates to them. By doing this, people can see the other person's viewpoint without passing judgment. They are then prompted to consider how they may address the problem from that point on. Students will first bargain on the most straightforward conditions.

Usually, one student will make a suggestion, and the other will accept it. Students soon pick up on more complicated negotiating techniques, problem-solving techniques, and reaching a win-win conclusion. Rena Arcaro-research McPhee's shown that when kids go through this process, they finally learn to settle disagreements on their own. Giving children the means to tackle their issues ought to be the final objective.

Additional suggestions for settling disputes include:

1. Communicate Your Emotions "Hey! I dislike seeing individuals getting shoved.
2. Teach Your Child to Make Changes: "I believe you startled Harry a little bit when you swung that stick close to him. What can we do to improve his mood? Do you believe he would like to play with us?

3. Provide an Option: We're going to put the slide on hold for the time being. I can tell you don't want to wait for your turn. You may play in the sandpit or swing on the swings. What are you interested in doing?

4. Act Without Insulting: We are leaving for home. On another day, we'll try the playground. I'm currently too concerned about injuries to youngsters.

5. Try to solve problems:

Recognize your child's emotions in the first step by saying, "I can tell that you don't enjoy me gripping your hand while we're in the parking lot. Your fingers feel constricted as a result.

Step two: State the issue: "The issue is, I worry about automobiles striking kids in the parking lot."

 Step Three: Request suggestions "We need some solutions so we can get everyone back to the vehicle safely,"

Step Four: Select the concepts that both of you find appealing. "So you enjoy the notion of bringing me to the vehicle while clutching onto my sleeve? I'd want to circle that one.

<u>Step Five</u>: Try several options "Here we are at the parking lot; why don't you hang onto my sleeve and show me the way!"

Try them out, and be sure to let the early childhood educator **know how it goes!**

# Chapter 3

How to praise and acknowledge your child

Finding the right balance in how to express our pride in our children may be challenging. Children get depressed when they receive little praise. They may become unbearably conceited if you give them too many compliments.

Finding the right balance between praise and displays of joy in our children's achievements may be challenging. These suggestions might assist parents in determining the proper method for giving praise and expressing delight in their children's work and successes.

1 . Congratulate them on the important things:

Every day, our kids get to experience new things, some of which are more significant than others. A high amount of praise is acceptable, for instance, if a youngster participated in piano performance, worked hard, practiced daily, selected a challenging piece, and considerably improved.

On the other side, parents may not want to be too complimentary if the piano student sucked at the performance because they didn't practice, didn't prepare, or picked a piece that was too easy.

Make sure to show your admiration for noteworthy efforts, but refrain from doing so excessively when it is not warranted.

2. Honor the procedure

Jane, a member of the high school tennis team, recently triumphed in the championship doubles match of the regional competition. Although her parents could congratulate her on winning the tournament match, saying "we are very proud of you" would not be the best response. She could think that victory is all that matters.

"Doesn't it feel nice to know that all of that practice, and effort to develop paid off," they would say? Not just for the victory, but also for all that went into it, Jane will feel validated. She won't simply feel fortunate to have won; she will also experience genuine personal joy at having succeeded.

3. Discuss Obstacles

Children often have to overcome challenges or problems to achieve anything in their life. Perhaps they had to give up certain things, like time with friends, to practice or improve their abilities. Perhaps they had some early defeats in a contest that showed them where they needed to develop.

They can tell how long we have been watching and how much attention we paid to their efforts along the road when we show joy in their achievement while also acknowledging the obstacles they had to face.

## 4. Speak with Confidence

By letting them know that we are proud of their successes and that they should be too, bragging about our kids' success may be beneficial for them. Much better messages for youngsters to hear and retain are those that indicate confidence in their abilities—if a child did something well, she can do many things well—and gratitude for the work they put into the experience.

## 5. Avoid going overboard

It's crucial to keep your displays of pride in perspective. Kids naturally understand the relative importance of different aspects of their life. While scoring her first goals in a soccer match is an achievement worthy of some focus and attention, a large neighborhood celebration is probably not in order.

A modest family gathering (such as pizza or ice cream) and a fruitful talk about how to accomplish individual objectives with the family would be acceptable.

## 6. Pick the Right Moment

When it is given and received just after a task is completed, praise is most effective. Using our soccer instance, it would be beneficial to offer high fives during the game, but it would also be beneficial to celebrate with the family over ice cream that day rather than wait a week. The event's closeness to our home and the acknowledgment give it much more significance for our youngsters.

## 7. Steer clear of blacklists

We hide praise in the middle of negativity much too often in an attempt to avoid risking instilling vanity in our kids. "We are thrilled about your first soccer goal, even if you still need to work hard on your academics and don't make your bed every day. Congratulations!"

Don't mention the shortcomings; simply show your real delight in the task at hand.

8. Attempt "I'm Proud of"

The best course of action is to go from expressing "I am proud of you" to "I am proud of you." The focus of the achievement shifts subtly from being on the parent to being on the kid.

9. When praising them, concentrate on them

It might be simple for a parent to direct their child's proud gestures toward other people. "You could do so much more if all of your kids were more like Jane!" That strategy does not inspire confidence; instead, it concentrates on those who are not doing well.

10. Appreciate other people's efforts.

Helping kids understand how others contributed to their achievement is a smart strategy to keep them modest while also celebrating their successes. The youngster should be congratulated for their efforts after receiving a report card with all As, but you should also urge them to consider and thank others who contributed.

It might be polite to send a teacher or parent volunteer a brief thank-you message. The youngster will feel good about their achievement but yet realize that it is nearly always a team effort if you can make them recognize that many others work toward their success.